Nadim was at the airport with his mum and dad. They had been to America for a holiday. Now it was time to fly home.

Nadim's dad was nervous. 'I don't like flying,' he said. 'I hate taking off.'

'I don't hate it,' said Nadim. 'I love it.'

1

On the flight, there was a surprise for Nadim. The steward asked him if he wanted to see the controls.

Nadim was excited. He had always wanted to see the flight deck of an aeroplane.

'Oh brilliant!' he said. 'Yes, please!'

The steward took Nadim and his dad through the aeroplane.

'These planes are huge,' said Nadim.

'They hold about four hundred people,' said the steward.

'That's a lot of people in one plane,' said Nadim.

3

Nadim and his dad went on to the flight deck.

They met the captain.

'We're flying on auto-pilot,' said the captain.

'The plane is flying by itself.'

Nadim looked at all the controls.

'I'd like to be a pilot,' he said.

'It takes a long time to learn,' said the Captain.
'But what's to stop you?'

'Don't let him take over the controls just yet,'
joked Nadim's dad. 'I'm a nervous passenger.'

'Oh Dad!' said Nadim.

After Nadim got home, he went to play at Biff and Chip's house.

Anneena was already there.

Nadim told everyone about his holiday. 'I went on to the flight deck of the aeroplane,' he said.

'I'd love to be a pilot,' said Anneena.

Mum called Biff and Chip. They had to go
downstairs to help wash up.

'We won't be long,' said Chip.

Anneena picked up the magic key. Suddenly it
began to glow.

It took Anneena and Nadim on an adventure.

The magic took Nadim and Anneena back in time. It took them to a place in America.

'Why has the magic key brought us here?' asked Anneena.

They heard the sound of an engine. The sound was coming out of a big cloud of dust.

8

A man was driving towards them in a strange-looking car.

'What on earth is it?' asked Nadim. 'It looks like a really old car.'

'You can't stand there!' called the man. 'You'll be in the way of the flying machine.'

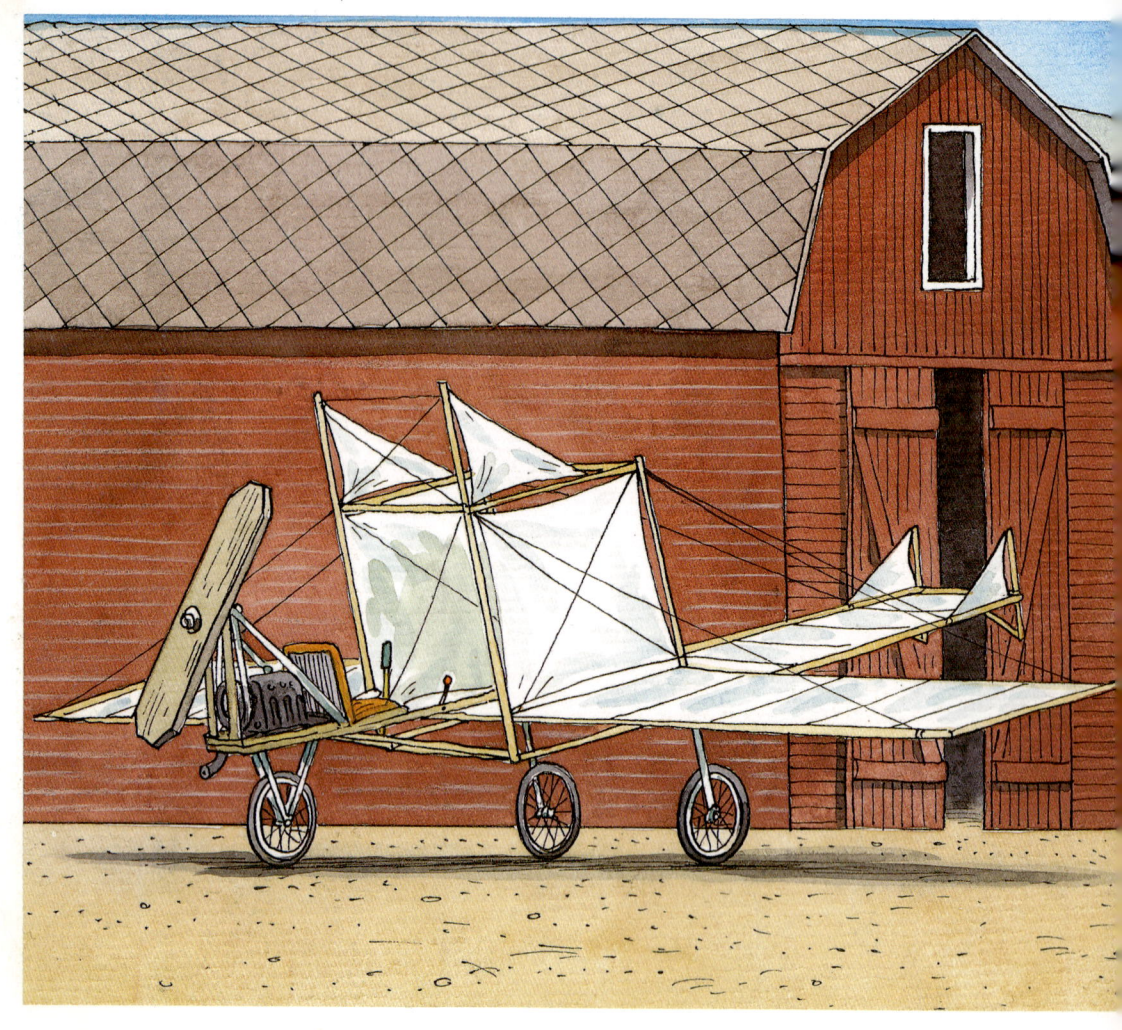

A strange-looking aeroplane was standing by a barn. Nadim and Anneena had never seen anything like it.

Another man was working on the aeroplane.

The first man got out of the car and went over to him.

10

Anneena gasped. The two men looked alike. 'They must be twins,' she said to Nadim.

'Hello,' said the second man. 'I'm Henry and this is my twin brother, Harold. Who are you?'

'I'm Nadim. This is Anneena,' said Nadim.

'You're not spying on us, are you?' asked Harold.

'Why would we do that?' asked Anneena.

'We're just about to try out the flying machine,' said Henry, 'but it's a secret.'

'No one has ever made a flying machine before,' said Harold. 'We will be the first people to do it.'

12

'It's amazing,' said Nadim. 'We've not seen an aeroplane like this before.'

The twins laughed. 'A hairy plane,' said Harold. 'That's a good name for it – a hairy plane!'

'But it will never fly,' said Anneena.

'Of course it will,' said Henry.

Harold sat in the flying machine. 'I'm ready!' he shouted.

Henry started the engine.

The propeller began to turn. It spun faster and faster. But the flying machine didn't move.

'I told you so,' said Anneena.

14

'It's the propeller,' said Anneena. 'It will never work. It's too flat.'

She picked up two pieces of wood.

'It needs to be like this,' she said. 'It acts like a screw to pull the plane through the air.'

'Well, we could try it,' said Henry.

The twins changed the shape of the propeller.

'But it still won't fly,' said Nadim. 'You only have a flat wing. You have no way to make it lift up. How will it take off?'

'Ha!' said Harold. 'We've made a ramp! The faster we go, the higher it will fly.'

16

Harold got into the aeroplane. Henry started the engine. 'We'll see if you're right,' he yelled.

The propeller spun round and the aeroplane began to move faster and faster.

'It's working!' shouted Henry.

'It still won't fly,' said Nadim.

17

The plane zoomed up the ramp at full speed. It rose in the air like a heavy bird.

'Yee-ha!' called Henry. 'It's flying.'

The plane flew straight up. It went backwards in a loop. Then it dived towards the ground.

'Help!' yelled Harold.

The plane hit the ground with a heavy bump.
Harold was thrown out.

It was still going at full speed. It roared towards
Nadim and Anneena.

'Stop it!' yelled Harold.

'Look out!' shouted Henry.

No one could stop the plane. It headed towards a big water tank.

'It's going to crash!' gasped Nadim.

The plane went under the water tank. The wings snapped off, but the plane went on.

'It hasn't stopped,' said Henry.

The plane didn't slow down. It roared on towards a farm.

Harold and Henry jumped into their car and chased after it.

'One thing's for sure,' said Nadim to Anneena, 'your propeller works well.'

Henry and Harold's mother and father lived on the farm.

Their mother had just done the washing. She was hanging it out to dry.

Their father was watering his prize melons and pumpkins.

Henry and Harold followed. Nadim and Anneena
chased after them.

'Aw heck!' said Harold. 'Why won't it stop?'

'Oh my!' said Henry. 'It's heading for the farm.'

'Oh dear,' said Anneena. 'I don't like the look of
this.'

The plane roared on.

It ran through the washing. It squashed the melons and pumpkins.

'It hasn't stopped,' shouted Harold. 'Now what are we going to do?'

'Let's hope it runs out of gas soon,' said Henry.

The plane headed towards the town.

A woman was painting her house. She heard the sound of an engine.

'Whatever is that?' she wondered. 'It sounds like a roaring bull.'

The plane ran into the ladder and knocked it
down.

The woman fell to the ground. She still had the
paint brush in her hand.

The plane went on.

'What the heck was that?' gasped the woman.

At last the plane stopped in the middle of the town.
It had crashed into a statue.

People ran to see what all the noise was about.

Henry and Harold stopped the car. They both
jumped out.

'This doesn't look good,' said Harold.

Nadim and Anneena ran to see where the plane
had stopped.

Nadim spoke to Harold and Henry.

'You see!' he said. 'The propeller works. Now you
need to make flaps and a rudder.'

Suddenly there was a noise. It sounded like an engine. It came from up in the sky.

Everyone looked up. An aeroplane was flying over the town.

'It's a flying machine!' someone shouted.

'Another hairy plane,' joked Anneena.

The people waved and cheered. The pilot of the plane waved back at them.

'I know who that is,' called a man. 'It's Wilbur Wright. He and his brother are the first men to fly.'

'Well I'll be darned!' said Henry.

'So we aren't the first men to fly after all,' said
Henry. 'The Wright brothers have beaten us to it.'

'Never mind,' said Harold. 'I have an idea for a
boat that goes under the water.'

The magic key began to glow. It was time for
Nadim and Anneena to go.

'Sorry we were such a long time,' said Biff. 'There was a lot of washing up to do.'

'Never mind,' laughed Anneena. 'The time just flew by.'

'And it wasn't just the time that flew,' joked Nadim.